Late Elementary thro ... Repertoire

AN INTRODUCTION TO SUCCEEDING WITH THE MASTERS®

Compiled and edited by Helen Marlais

About the Book

In this book, students discover works by the master composers from the Baroque, Classical, and Romantic eras. To ensure authenticity, all of these pieces have been extensively researched. After completing this book, students will be ready for *Succeeding with the Masters*®–a series dedicated to the authentic keyboard works of the Baroque, Classical, Romantic, and Twentieth-Century masters. The entire series brings together an essential and comprehensive library of the pedagogical repertoire of the great composers.

The entire *Succeeding with the Masters*® series provides a complete and easily accessible method to learning and performing the works of the masters. Each book presents the works in historical perspective for the student, and provides the means and the motivation to play these pieces in the correct stylistic, musical, and technical manner. The easily understandable format of practice strategies and musical concepts makes this series enjoyable for both students and teachers.

Teachers will find a wealth of excellent repertoire that can be used for recitals, festivals, competitions, and state achievement testing. Many of these original compositions will probably be new to you and some will be quite familiar. Upon completion of this series, students will be well prepared for the major keyboard works by the master composers of each era.

Production: Frank J. Hackinson
Production Coordinator: Joyce Loke
Cover: Terpstra Design, San Francisco
Text Design and Layout: Susan Pinkerton and Terpstra Design
Cover and Interior Art Concepts: Helen Marlais
Interior Illustrations: © 2009 Susan Hellard/Arena
Cover: Chalk lithograph of J. S. Bach from the *Pougin Iconography Collection*, Sibley Music Library
Engraving: Tempo Music Press, Inc.
Printer: Tempo Music Press, Inc

ISBN 1-56939-714-7

AN INTRODUCTION TO SUCCEEDING WITH THE MASTERS®

A Note for Teachers and Students

An Introduction to Succeeding with the Masters® is a collection of repertoire of the late elementary through early intermediate levels that features the great masters of the Baroque, Classical, and Romantic eras. These works build a foundation for playing more music by the master composers in *Succeeding with the Masters®*. Many of the pieces are introduced with a short "discovery" of a particular characteristic of the era. "Practice strategies" guide the student in preparing and performing each piece. This comprehensive approach to learning style, technique, and historical context provides a valuable foundation for successful performance of all repertoire pieces.

The following icons are used throughout the volume:

These icons indicate musical characteristics of the eras

Characteristics of the Baroque Era

Characteristics of the Classical Era

Characteristics of the Romantic Era

Practice Strategy

This icon outlines a practice strategy or illustrates a musical concept that guides the student in how to learn more efficiently and play more musically.

The pieces in this collection are based on facsimiles of the composer's own manuscripts and on Urtext editions, which are editions that reflect the composer's original intent. From these scores, the editor has created performance scores for the student.

- Editorial metronome markings are added as a guide.
- Ornaments have been realized for the student and appear as ossias above the staff.
- Keep your CD close by! It includes complete performances and a practice strategy lesson for each piece. For a complete listing of track numbers, see the next page.

Different keyboards through history:

clavichord

harpsichord

pianoforte

Late Elementary through Early Intermediate Repertoire

TABLE OF CONTENTS

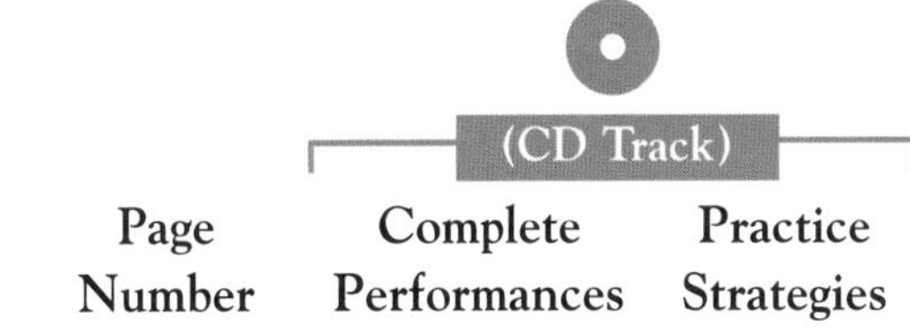

TIME LINE OF THE ERAS AND TH

THE BAROQUE ERA

c.1600–c.1750

Johann Sebastian Bach is behind the harpsichord.
George Frideric Handel is in front of the harpsichord.
Domenico Scarlatti is sitting at the harpsichord.

THE CLASSICAL ERA

c.1750–c.1820

Franz Joseph Haydn is sitting at the pianoforte.
Ludwig van Beethoven is behind the pianoforte.
Wolfgang Amadeus Mozart is in front of the pianoforte

N.B. c. is the abbreviation for *circa*. It means *approximately*.

THE ROMANTIC ERA

c.1800–c.1900

Franz Schubert is playing the piano.
Peter Tchaikovsky is behind the piano.
Robert Schumann is in front of the piano.

WHICH ERA IS WHICH?

- Draw a line from each picture below to the correct era on the left.

Musician performing during the Baroque era:

Musicians performing a string quartet during the classical era:

Two pianists performing a piano duet during the Romantic era:

THE MUSICAL CHARACTERISTICS

- **Draw a line from each era to match the correct image. Your teacher will help you decide.**

THE BAROQUE ERA

The music and art of the Baroque era is highly ornamented, and always appears to be in motion. Notice that the style fills the space with action and movement.

THE CLASSICAL ERA

The music and art of the Classical era is symmetrical and well-balanced.

OF EACH ERA

THE ROMANTIC ERA

Romantic music often tells a story or creates a mood.

Other Characteristics of the Eras:

BAROQUE PIECES

- rhythm is very important, with a steady beat and regular accents
- the minuet was a popular dance
- binary or rounded binary form was used
- phrases are irregular lengths
- rhythmic and melodic patterns were repeated
- ornamentations (trills, turns, etc.) were used
- the right and left hands have interesting melodies in the same piece

CLASSICAL PIECES

- melodies are easy to sing along with and recognize
- phrases are often four measures long, well-balanced and symmetrical
- the right hand often has a melody and the left hand provides the harmony
- traditional classical forms are used: binary, rounded binary, and ternary

ROMANTIC PIECES

- many pieces have titles that create an image in the mind of the listener
- emotion and drama are important
- phrases are of varying lengths
- tempos change within the same piece (*ritardando*, *rubato*)

The Baroque Masters

Johann Sebastian Bach was a church organist and music director. He could play the harpsichord, violin, clavichord, and organ, as well as the violin! Bach was born in 1685 in Germany.

George Frideric Handel was known for writing operas, keyboard music, and oratorios. Oratories are Bible stories set to music and a famous one written by Handel is *The Messiah.* Handel was also born in 1685 in Germany.

Domenico Scarlatti was the court composer for the Queen of Spain. He wrote over 550 sonatas for the keyboard and was a dazzling keyboard player! Scarlatti was also born in 1685, but in Italy.

MINUET IN G MINOR

This piece was written before the year 1707, when Bach visited the German town of Lübeck, which was inspiring to him because of the many evening concerts.

Use of the popular minuet:

Characteristics of the Baroque Era

The minuet is a dance of French origin, usually in triple meter, to be played at a moderate to brisk tempo. The minuet evolved in tempo and style from the Baroque through Classical eras but remained popular with the upper class until the late eighteenth century.

Many baroque pieces follow either a binary or rounded binary form.

Binary
(two parts, different melodic material in each section)

Rounded Binary
(when part of the A section returns in the B section)

Characteristics of the Baroque Era

Looking at the full score, this Minuet has what form? Mark with a star ★ the A section, mark with an X the B section, and if you see the A section return in your score, mark it with a star ★ .

Practicing with the metronome:

Practice Strategy

This technique not only helps you to play evenly and steadily, but it also helps you to give each note its full durational value, which is extremely important in playing baroque music. Since each note must be articulated with the best possible clarity and focus, consistent practice with the metronome will guide you in becoming a good player!

Always remember that rhythm is a distinctive element of the Baroque era, and keeping a steady beat with regular accents is very important.

Set the metronome at ♩ = M.M. 60. Practice hands separately at first, then hands together. When you are comfortable with this speed, you can increase it. Once you can do this easily, set the metronome at 60 to the 𝅗𝅥., feeling one beat per bar. This will help to create a dance-like minuet feel.

Remember, the metronome helps you develop an inner pulse!

MINUET IN G MINOR

Johann Sebastian Bach
BWV 822

(𝅗𝅥. = M.M. 60-69)

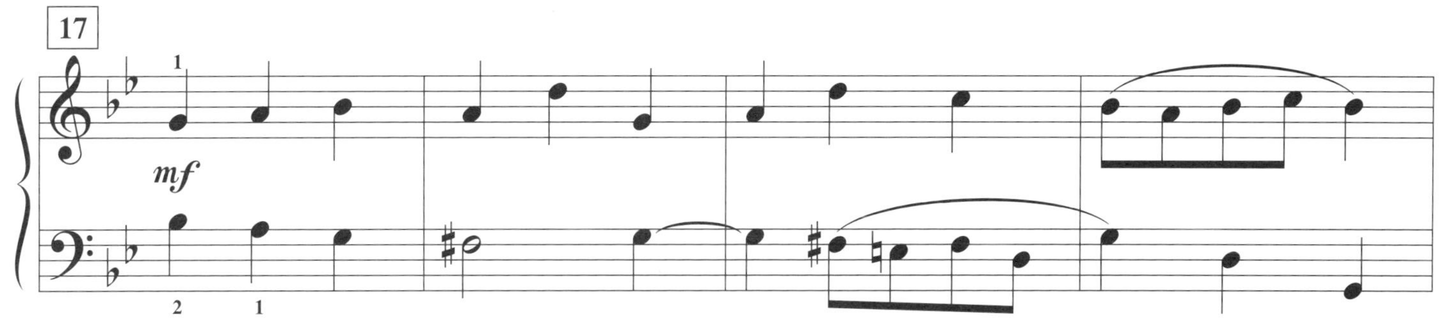
17
1
mf
2 1

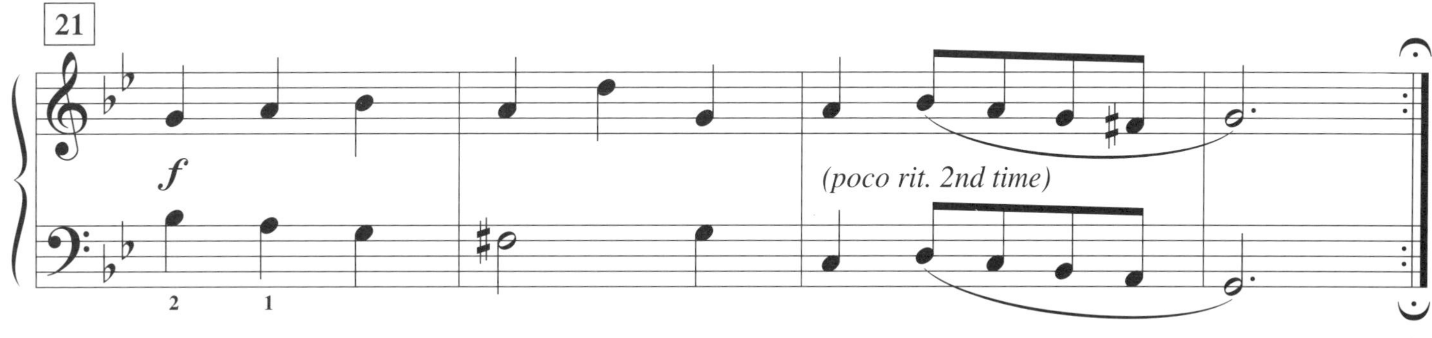
21
f
(poco rit. 2nd time)
2 1

IMPERTINENCE

This piece has an interesting title. When you listen to the CD recording, look up the definition of the word in a dictionary.

Characteristics of the Baroque Era

Characteristics of the era observed in this piece:

- Recurring rhythmic and melodic patterns
- Both sections of the piece end with an ornament that resolves to the last note.
- Use of a countermelody

Understanding countermelodies:

Sometimes an important melody is accompanied by a new melody, called a *countermelody*. Do you notice, in the example below, that the melody in the right hand begins, and then the left-hand melody begins before the right hand has finished? The same occurs in measures three and four. The countermelodies in the left hand are being very insistent, as if it is a conversation. The left hand is even being a bit stubborn, coming in before the right hand has finished!

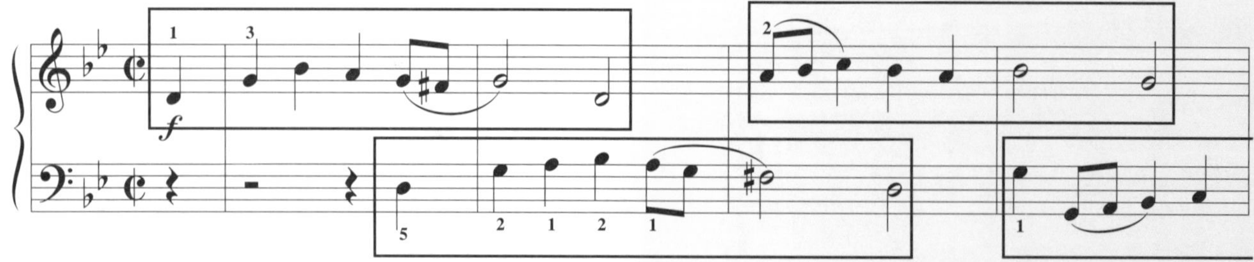

Practice Strategy

How to play baroque articulations:

Since the keyboard instruments of the era were very different from the modern-day piano, performers had different concerns that we must carefully consider.

Experiment in the following ways:
Lightly accent every quarter note in the piece that is followed by eighth notes. To accent, play in a semi-detached manner, with a fine and slight emphasis of the notes. First, play the quarter notes semi-detached, and then play them all with a *staccato* touch. Do you hear the difference in the articulation?

First play:

Then play:

Then, for every eighth-note pattern, try not to force the first note. Instead, a small *crescendo* through the second eighth note all the way to the longest note of the short phrase is best. This will help to give the piece energy and rhythmic drive.

IMPERTINENCE

George Frideric Handel
HWV 494

(a) Optional trills: or or (b)

Minuet in G minor

Practice Strategy

Bringing a piece to life musically after it is learned:

In order to bring a piece to life for an audience, the tempo, the articulations, and the dynamics must be accurate. Listen to the recording of this piece, and think about the following musical ideas:

1) The tempo

Set your metronome at the following three tempos. Start at different places in the piece and concentrate on the steadiness of the beat throughout.

Which tempo feels the best to you?

2) The articulations

The different articulations between the hands make this piece interesting. Play the piece four times, each time paying careful attention to only *one* of the following points:

1) The lilt at the end of each three-note slur in the right hand. ❐

2) Every eighth note played in a detached, *non legato* style. ❐

3) Giving a little space between the quarter and eighth-note figures in the left hand. ❐

4) The *legato* sound played only within the slurs. ❐

Check each box when you are sure you have focused on that particular point, and have played the entire piece with this in mind.

3) The dynamics

C.P. E. Bach, one of J.S. Bach's sons, wrote an *Essay on the True Art of Playing Keyboard Instruments*, which is still read by performers today. He wrote that it was important to play dynamics tastefully and that they should reflect the overall mood of the piece. Circle the one adjective which best illustrates this piece:

energetic	*lonely*	*cheerful*
perky	*harsh*	*sweet*

Minuet in G minor

Domenico Scarlatti
K. 88d/L. 36

(a) All eighth notes may be played *non legato*, unless marked otherwise.

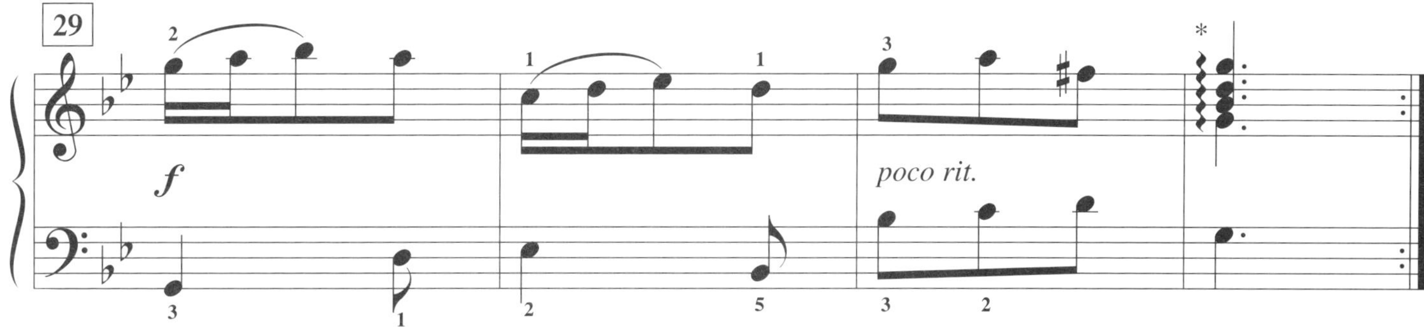

*The roll is editorial.

Picture of a musician singing.
Notice the baroque clothing of the musician and the highly ornamented room where he stands.
From *The Universal Musician*, 1731.

The Classical Masters

Franz Joseph Haydn worked for a royal family named Esterházy. The musicians he worked with respected and loved him so much they nicknamed him "Papa Haydn." This is a picture of the palace in which he lived and worked.

Wolfgang Amadeus Mozart toured Europe with his sister when they were young, playing many concerts. He wrote operas, symphonies, piano works, and chamber music. Mozart was a friend of Haydn's and dedicated some of his compositions to him.

Ludwig van Beethoven wrote many famous works, including nine symphonies, thirty-two piano sonatas, and five piano concertos. He began going deaf at the age of 31.

Haydn was born on March 31, 1732, in Austria.

Mozart was born on January 27, 1756, in Austria.

Beethoven was born on December 16, 1770, in Germany.

German Dance No. 8 in G major

The German Dance in G is from the collection of twelve minuets for the *Clavecin* or *Piano Forte*

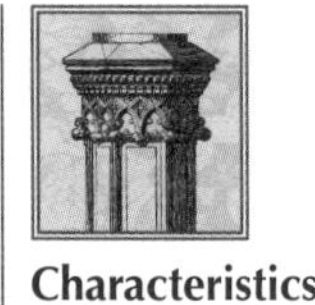

Characteristics of the Classical Era

This dance is in binary form – AB (meaning "two parts"). The A section ends on the dominant (D7), while the B section ends on the tonic (G major). Label these two parts, AB, in your score.

Melodic motives were short and repetitive during the Classical era. This is one reason why melodies were so easy to recognize and sing along with.

In the excerpt below, find and circle the short melodic motive that looks like this: (The first one is done for you.)

Practice Strategy

How many times does this motive occur in this dance? ____________________

Shaping the two-note slurs in this dance is essential. To do so, let your wrist drop and let your finger sink to the bottom of the key on the first note of each motive (denoted with a downward arrow).

As you begin to play the last note of the two-note slur, lift your wrist and roll up on your fifth finger until you are playing on its fingertip. Move your wrist and arm towards the fallboard of the piano (denoted with the upward arrow above).

The second note of the slur should sound lighter than the first note. Let your wrist fall and drop onto the next quarter note. Practice this technique until secure and comfortable.

German Dance No. 8 in G major

Franz Joseph Haydn
Hob. IX: 8, No. 8

(a) The top C may be omitted if played by a smaller hand.
(b) The low D may be omitted if played by a smaller hand.

Minuet in C

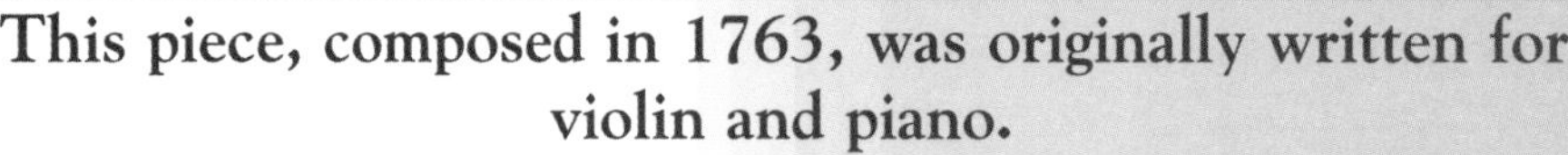

This piece, composed in 1763, was originally written for violin and piano.

Characteristics of the Classical Era

Observe in this Minuet:

- melodic motives are short and repetitive
- frequent use of two-note slurs

Practice Strategy

"Chain-linking" practice helps to increase accuracy and solidity.

Here's how it works:

Stop here, on beat two.

Play beats one and two.
Stop on the second beat!
Repeat until easy.
This practice strategy is to be used at a slow, "thinking" tempo.
Listen for the clarity of the two-note slur and the balance between the hands.

Add another "link" onto the chain:
Play from the first beat to the downbeat of measure seven.
As you continue to add one or two beats to the chain, the phrase will become longer and you will feel its forward motion.

Stop on the downbeat of measure seven.

Use the "chain-linking" strategy for up to *three measures* of music.

Shaping the phrases:

Looking at the full score, circle one phrase goal in the A section. This phrase goal is the place towards which the music naturally moves. Let your ear be your guide and listen to this rise of melody towards the goal. After this goal, the phrase naturally tapers. Play the phrases in the B section, again listening for the phrase goal.

Minuet in C

Wolfgang Amadeus Mozart
K 6

* The brackets have been added to show the long line of the phrase.

German Dance in C major

This German Dance, No. 1 of a set of 12, was written in 1795 when the composer was 25 years old. Since Beethoven taught many students himself, this set was probably used as teaching repertoire.

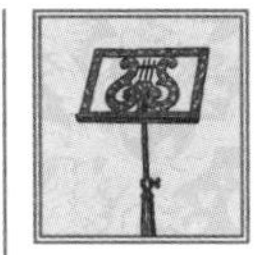

Practice Strategy

Practicing two-note slurs:

The thirds in measures 10 and 12 must be played *legato* (connected). To do this, on beat two of measure 10, lift the second finger while holding onto the upper note, as seen in the example below. Then prepare for the quarter notes by moving fingers 1 and 2 over these notes.

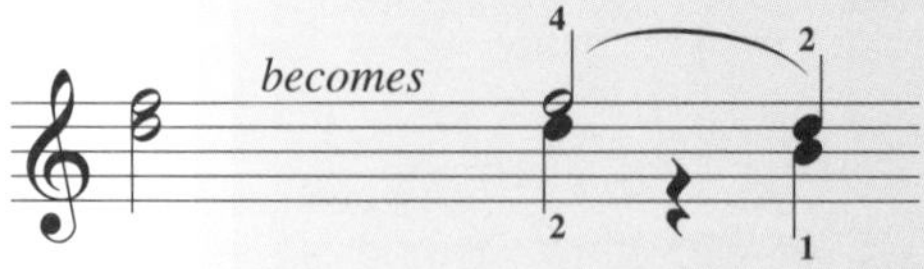

Practice Strategy

In order to play scale passages quickly and accurately, use "impulse" practicing.
Here are four easy steps:

1) Break a phrase into short segments.
For example, play beats one to two, *a tempo*, listening for evenness.
This short segment played quickly as well as accurately, is called an "impulse."

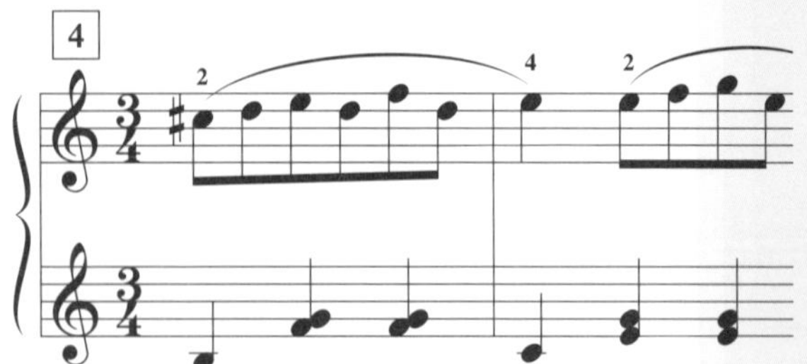

2) Then practice beats one to three in the same manner.

3) Then practice the whole measure to beat one of the next measure, still playing quickly as one impulse.

4) Start impulse practice on any downbeat, but add onto it only short segments.

German Dance in C major

Ludwig van Beethoven
WoO 8

(♩ = m.m. 152-192)

(a) The upper notes may be omitted if played by a smaller hand.

The Romantic Masters

Franz Schubert was known for writing beautiful melodies. He wrote over 600 songs for voice and piano! When he was young, he sang in a famous boys' choir in Vienna, Austria. Schubert was born on January 31, 1797, in Austria.

Robert Schumann is considered to be the "poet" of the piano. His first works were all for the piano. He married a concert pianist named Clara and they had seven children. Schumann was born on June 8, 1810, in Germany.

Pyotr Ilyich Tchaikovsky saw an opera at the age of ten and he knew then that music was what he would do for the rest of his life. His ballet, *The Nutcracker*, often performed at Christmastime, is one of his most famous works. Tchaikovsky was born on May 7, 1840, in Russia.

SOLDIERS' MARCH

This piece and all of the pieces by Schumann in this volume are from a collection entitled *Album for the Young*. The same year this collection was composed, revolutions occurred throughout Europe.

Some pieces are programmatic, which means that they tell a story, or create an image in the mind of the listener that relates to the title. This piece definitely sounds like the title, because the dotted rhythms create the feel of a march.

Characteristics of the Romantic Era

How to create a march:

Practice Strategy

A march has simple and strong rhythm, and regular phrasing. In order to feel this piece as a march, one must be sure that it is rhythmically accurate.

1) Tap and speak the subdivisions of the first measure, no faster than ♩ = MM. 66.

Right hand: 

Left hand: 

one (e and) a - two

2) Play the first measure without the slur and speak the subdivisions:

3) Practice all of the measures with dotted rhythms in the same way.

4) Then play complete four-measure phrases with the slurs as written. Continue to speak the subdivisions and play with the metronome.

5) Remember that silences/rests are just as important as the notes you play. Speaking the subdivisions will help to keep the rests the correct length.

6) Next, play without speaking the subdivisions, but keep the metronome on. Ask yourself, "Does my rhythm sound like a march, with perfectly dotted rhythms and a steady beat?"

SOLDIERS' MARCH

Robert Schumann
Op. 68, No. 2

N.B. All eighth notes should be played *staccato*. The slurs are editorial as well as < and >.

N.B. The dynamic markings in measures 19 and 21 are editorial.

ÉCOSSAISE IN C MAJOR

An *écossaise* is a country dance played in a quick $\frac{2}{4}$ meter. This piece is from a set of eight *écossaises,* composed in Austria on October 3, 1815. Elsewhere in the world, the first commercial cheese factory was opened in Switzerland.

Characteristics of the Romantic Era

Some romantic composers, Schubert among them, enjoyed using traditional forms. Many of Schubert's écossaises have a binary form (AB). Mark AB in your score (with a pencil!).

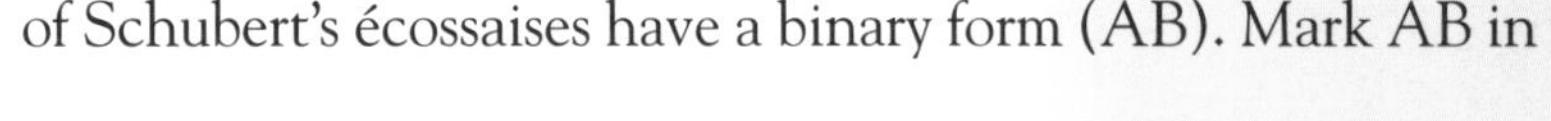

Practice Strategy

The importance of "hands-alone" work:

As you begin learning this piece, practice it hands apart. If any of the reaches are too large for your hands, omit the notes that are in parentheses. You can choose your fingering once you and your teacher decide what to do about these particular notes.

Measures 7-8, left hand:
Do these two measures feel better with or without the lower G on the second beat?

Measure 16, right hand:
Is this measure easier to play with or without the lower C on the first beat?

Let the phrase marks be a guide for you when you practice hands separately. By concentrating on the phrasing, the fingering will make a great deal of sense, because within each slur you will see a pattern.

Similar pattern, starting 1 step higher.

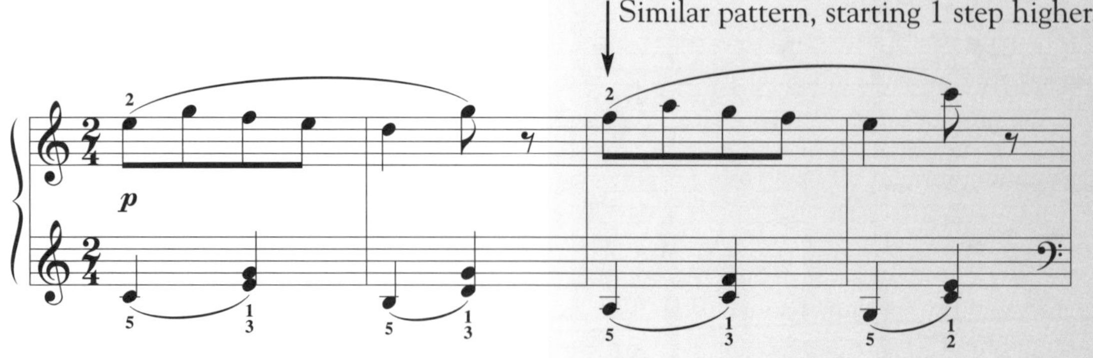

Écossaise in C major

Franz Schubert
D. 299, No. 8

(a) The low G may be omitted if played by a smaller hand.

N.B. The long slurs in measures 5–8, 9–10, and 13–14 show the longer phrases and are editorial.

The New Doll

This is the third and happiest piece about dolls in Tchaikovsky's *Children's Album*. In the year this piece was composed, electricity in homes was becoming more common.

Characteristics of the Romantic Era

Characteristics of the era exemplified in this piece:

- Phrases of varying lengths
- *The New Doll* is programmatic, which means that the energetic melody and rhythm of the piece create an image related to the title.

Practice Strategy

Shaping phrases:

This lively piece is made up of both long and short phrases. The dynamic markings in the long phrases show you where the phrase goals are. (A phrase goal is the place towards which the music naturally moves. In other words, the high point of the phrase is the phrase goal.)

Take a look at measures 17 to 25, listening to the CD. Notice that even though the short phrases are separated by rests, they form one long phrase which leads to the *forte* in measure 25. This is the high point of the entire piece. After this phrase goal is reached, the dynamics taper.

1 long phrase to the forte

Sometimes singing the melody can help guide you in knowing how to shape each phrase, and understand how each phrase leads to the next phrase.

Practice Strategy

How to play repeated notes quickly and lightly:

The left hand must be played quickly, quietly, evenly, and lightly. In order to achieve this technique, drop into the keys with a loose wrist on the first beat. On the next beat, pull up from the keys with your wrist until you are playing on your fingertips. The second beat should sound lighter than the first one. Practice your left hand separately until the gesture is secure and comfortable, and you will not get tired!

The New Doll

Pyotr Ilyich Tchaikovsky
Op. 39, No. 6

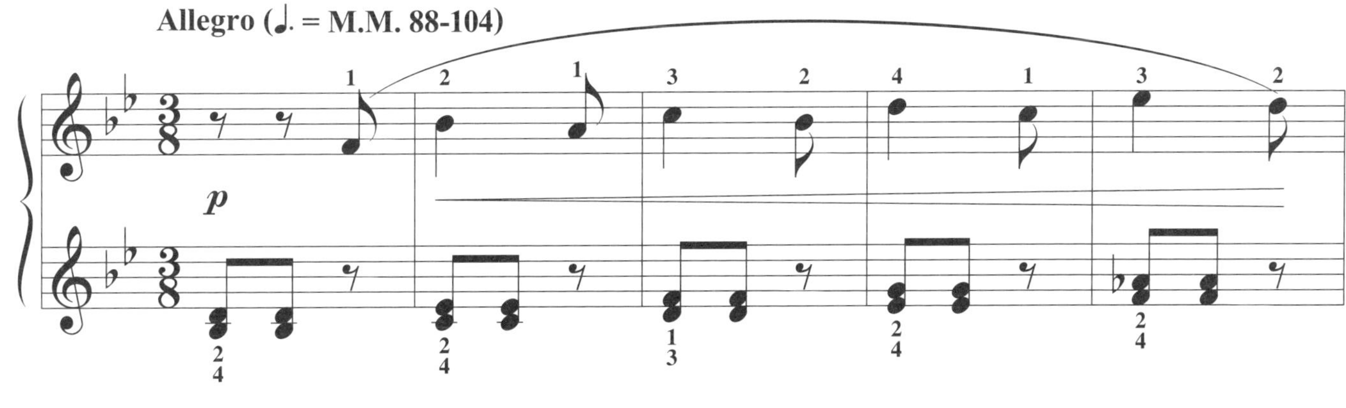

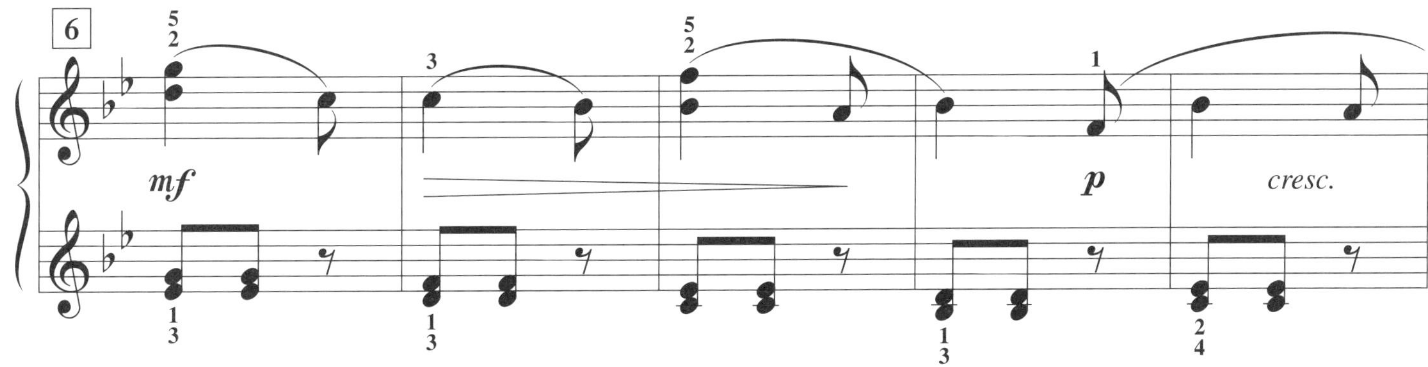

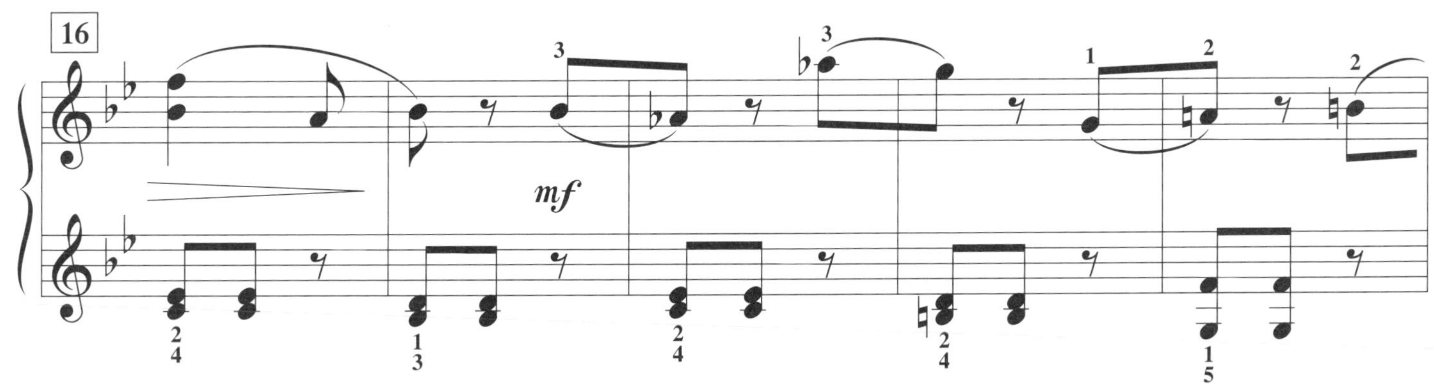

N.B. All L.H. eighth notes should be played *staccato*.
In measure 17, ***p*** is found in the Tchaikovsky's autograph copy, but it was changed to ***mf*** by an editor of the first edition. You can decide which you prefer!

21
cresc.
f
dim.
26
31
p
36
mf
p

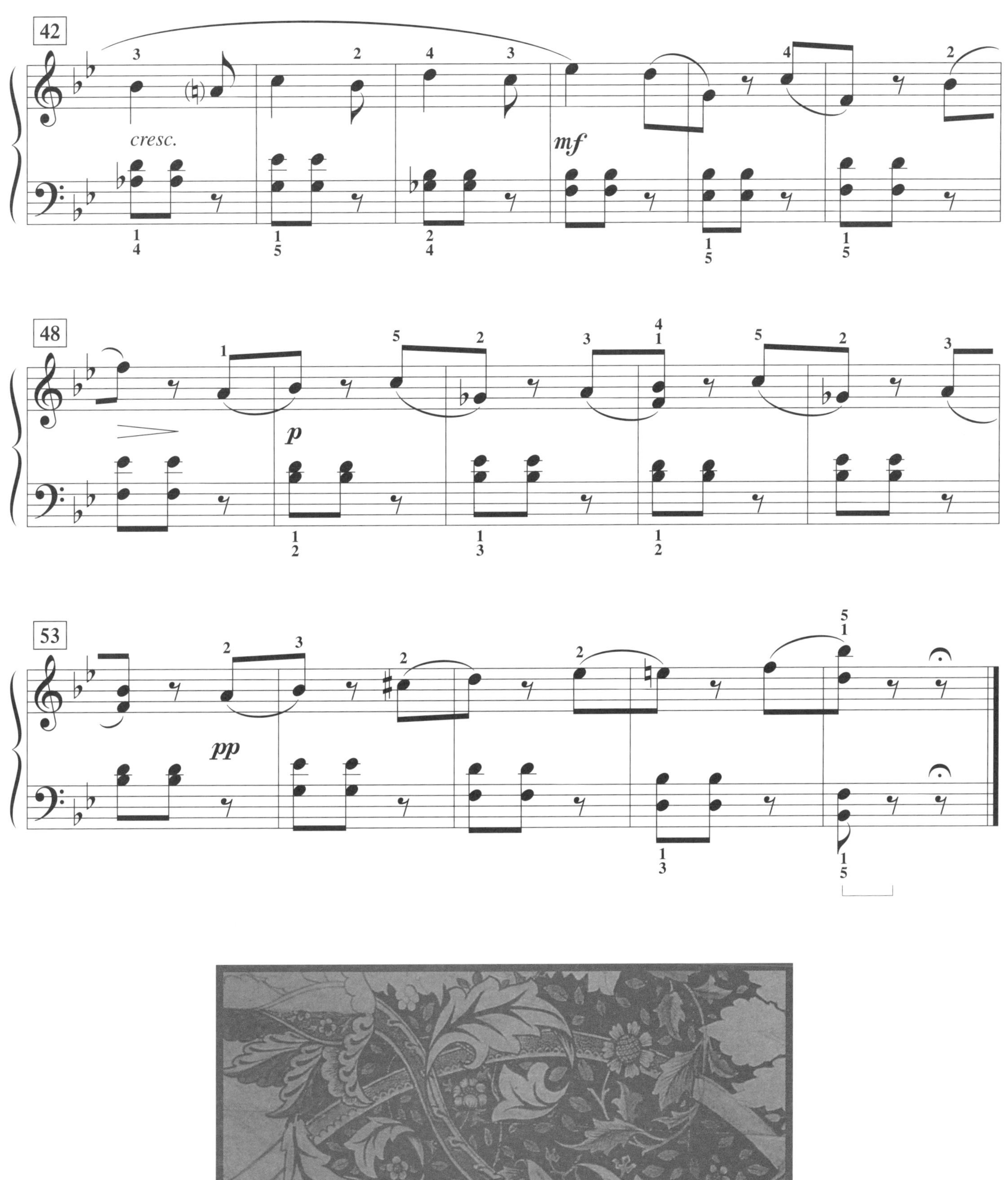
42
cresc.
mf
48
p
53
pp

Composers' Hall of Fame

- Draw a line from the composer's name to his picture on the next page. Your teacher will help you.

Johann Sebastian Bach

Wolfgang Amadeus Mozart

Pyotr Ilyich Tchaikovsky

George Frideric Handel

Franz Joseph Haydn

Robert Schumann

Domenico Scarlatti

Ludwig van Beethoven

Franz Schubert

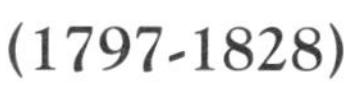

(1797-1828)

(1685-1750)

(1732-1809)

(1770-1827)

(1840-1893)

(1685-1759)

(1685-1757)

(1756-1791)

(1810-1856)

DICTIONARY

Accompaniment - a musical background for a principal part. The background may be the left hand of a keyboard composition or orchestral background for a solo instrument. The accompaniment provides harmony for the melody.

Articulation - the manner of playing; the touch. Refers to how notes are attacked, sustained, or accented—*legato, staccato,* etc.

a tempo - return to the regular tempo, especially after a *ritardando (rit.).*

Authentic cadence - a closing formula, usually two chords that move from the dominant chord (V) to the tonic (I).

Binary form - a piece built in two parts (AB); the first part sometimes ends on the tonic but most of the time ends on the dominant chord (V), and the second part ends on the tonic. Both parts are usually marked to be repeated before going on.

cantabile - an Italian term for "singing."

Countermelody - a musical line different from that of the primary melody. A countermelody can be part of an accompaniment.

Counterpoint - two melodies played simultaneously as different voices.

Downbeat - the first beat of a full measure, or the downward motion of a conductor's hand.

Écossaise - a quick country dance in 2/4 time.

Embellishment - also called ornamentation. The way composers fill out or decorate the texture, making the sound more grand.

fermata - means to hold the note longer than its full value.

Homophonic texture - a melody supported by harmonies. The melodic voice is often in the right hand with chords in the left, to create the harmony. It can also be done the other way around, melody in the left hand and chords above.

Imitation - when a melodic idea is heard in one voice and then heard in another voice.

Minuet - an elegant dance in triple meter, first introduced during the time of Louis XIV around the year 1650. It became a movement in the baroque suite.

Motive - a short melodic or rhythmic pattern (a few pitches) from which a full melodic and rhythmic phrase may grow.

Ornamentation - embellishment; the way composers fill out or decorate the texture, making the sound more grand.

Polyphonic texture - music with several lines (two or more) instead of a single melody and an accompaniment.

Programmatic music - when the title of a piece creates an image or a story for the listener. An example of this is, *Soldier's March* and *The New Doll*.

Rounded binary form- a piece in regular binary form, with one difference: the opening tune of the A section returns within the B section to lead back to a nice "rounded" conclusion for the piece.

rubato - the Italian word for "stolen," indicating to stretch or broaden the tempo. The time taken is made up within the same phrase or shortly thereafter.

sforzando - an Italian term (abbreviated ***sf***), which means to create a sudden, strong accent on a note or chord.

Tempo - the speed of a piece. Some important tempos are the following: *allegro*, *allegretto*, *moderato*, *andante*, *grave*.

Ternary form - music that has three sections, ABA or ABC.

Trill - an ornament consisting of a repetitive alternation of a note with the note a whole step or half step above it. The ornament usually begins above the principal note in the Baroque and Classical eras.

Upbeat - one or more notes in an incomplete measure occurring before the first bar line of a piece or section of music; sometimes called a *pickup*.

Congratulations!

____

(Student's Name)

You have completed

An Introduction to Succeeding with the Masters®

and are now ready for

Succeeding with the Masters®, Volume 1

Baroque, Classical, and Romantic Eras

________________________ ________________

(Teacher's Signature) (Date)